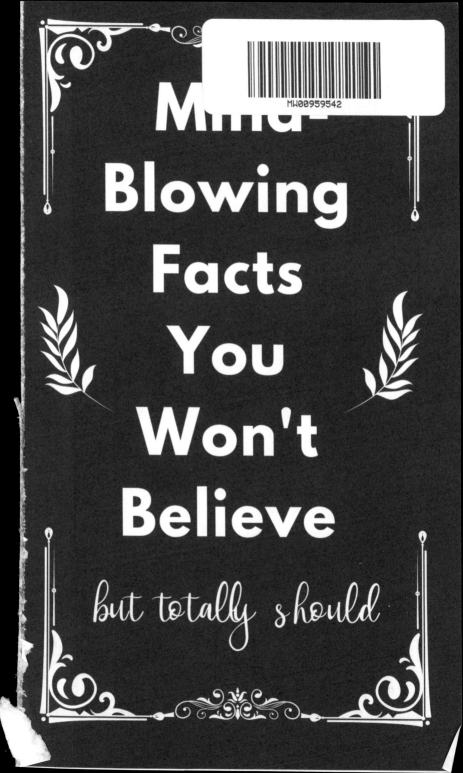

Mind-Blowing

Blowing

Facts

You

Won't

Believe

but totally should

Welcome to the Wacky World of Weirdness!

So, you've stumbled upon this book—congratulations! You're about to dive into a collection of some of the weirdest, funniest, and most bizarre facts the world has ever known. What's in here? Only the stuff legends (and crazy world records) are made of! This isn't your average trivia book—it's the ultimate conversation starter, boredom-buster, and brain-expander, all rolled into one. You'll learn about people who've balanced absurd numbers of spoons on their bodies, held their breath underwater for ridiculous amounts of time, and even sailed down rivers in giant pumpkins. Yeah, that's a thing. With 8 categories of pure madness, this book is packed with 48 mind-blowing, laugh-out-loud facts in each.

We're talking about:

- The strangest world records you've never heard of (Did someone actually eat 25 marshmallows in under a minute? Yes, yes they did).
- Animals behaving in ways that will make you question reality.
- History so odd you'll wonder if your history teacher was holding out on you.
- Sports and competitions so bizarre you'll be glad you stuck to normal hobbies.

Whether you're killing time, looking to impress your friends with the most ridiculous trivia, or simply need some quirky knowledge to share at your next party, this book has got your back. Plus, where else will you find facts about eating contests, weird animal talents, and a guy who broke the record for balancing a chainsaw on his chin?

By the end, you'll have more fun facts in your head than anyone else in the room—and possibly a few "wait, what?" moments along the way.

But hey, once you've finished this wild ride, do us a favor —leave an honest review! We'd love to hear what blew your mind, made you laugh, or had you questioning reality. We promise the facts are real... mostly.

Enjoy, have fun, and may your new knowledge make you the unofficial king or queen of random!

Weird World Records

FACT 1

The longest recorded burp lasted 1 minute and 13 seconds, achieved by an Italian man.

FACT 2

The world's largest pizza, made in Rome, measured 13,580 square feet.

FACT 3

A woman holds the record for the most Big Macs eaten in a lifetime—over 32,000.

FACT 4

The most spoons balanced on a face is 31, achieved by a man from Canada.

FACT 5

The longest fingernails ever measured belonged to a woman whose nails reached over 28 feet in length.

FACT 6

The largest rubber band ball weighed over 9,000 pounds and was made in Florida.

FACT 7

The most toilet seats broken by a head in one minute is 46.

FACT 8

The farthest distance to blow a pea with one breath is 24 feet and 7 inches.

FACT 9

The longest kiss lasted 58 hours, 35 minutes, and 58 seconds, set by a couple in Thailand.

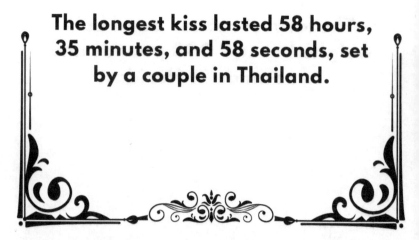

FACT 10

The world record for the most T-shirts worn at once is 260.

FACT 11

The most tattoos given in 24 hours by a single person is 801.

FACT 12

A man holds the record for the most live rattlesnakes held in his mouth—13.

FACT 13

The fastest time to eat a bowl of pasta is 26.69 seconds.

FACT 14

The largest gathering of people dressed as Smurfs is 2,762.

FACT 15

The longest time someone held their breath underwater is 24 minutes and 3 seconds.

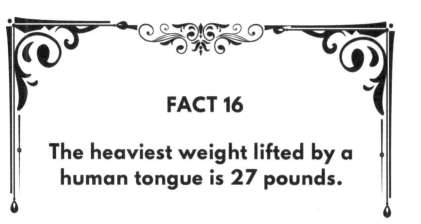

FACT 16

The heaviest weight lifted by a human tongue is 27 pounds.

FACT 17

The most people simultaneously hula-hooping is 4,483.

FACT 18

The most steps walked by a dog balancing a glass of water on its head is 10.

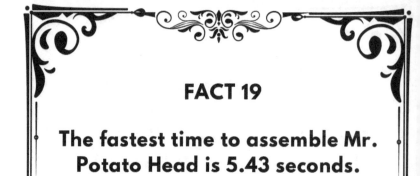

FACT 19

The fastest time to assemble Mr. Potato Head is 5.43 seconds.

FACT 20

A man holds the record for fitting 264 straws in his mouth at once.

FACT 21

The longest time spent controlling a soccer ball with the feet while walking up stairs is 4 minutes and 19 seconds.

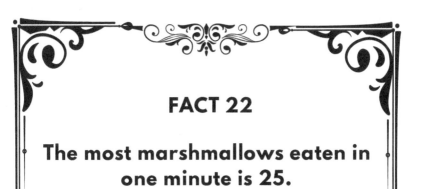

FACT 22

The most marshmallows eaten in one minute is 25.

FACT 23

The record for the most spoons balanced on a human body is 85.

FACT 24

The largest collection of rubber ducks totals over 9,000.

FACT 25

A man holds the record for having 516 bees on his body at once.

FACT 26

The tallest stack of doughnuts ever created reached 3.6 meters (12 feet) high.

FACT 27

The most people doing the worm dance simultaneously is 1,069.

FACT 28

The fastest time to carve a pumpkin is **16.47 seconds.**

FACT 29

The longest time spinning a basketball on a toothbrush is **1 minute and 8 seconds.**

FACT 30

The most Jenga blocks stacked on one vertical block is **485.**

FACT 31

The longest time balancing a chainsaw on the chin is 10 minutes and 56 seconds.

FACT 32

The largest pillow fight ever involved over 7,600 people.

FACT 33

The most clothes pegs clipped to a face in one minute is 51.

FACT 34

The largest human mattress dominoes event had 2,016 participants.

FACT 35

The world record for the longest hair on a teenager is over 5 feet long.

FACT 36

The largest bubblegum bubble ever blown measured 20 inches in diameter.

FACT 37

The fastest marathon run in a fruit costume (banana) is 2 hours, 47 minutes.

FACT 38

The most people simultaneously cracking eggs is 1,173.

FACT 39

The longest conga line had 119,986 people.

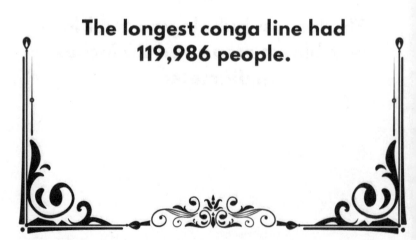

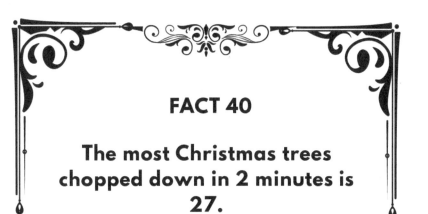

FACT 40

The most Christmas trees chopped down in 2 minutes is 27.

FACT 41

The largest gathering of people dressed as penguins is 624.

FACT 42

Fact: The most tattooed man has 99.9% of his body inked.

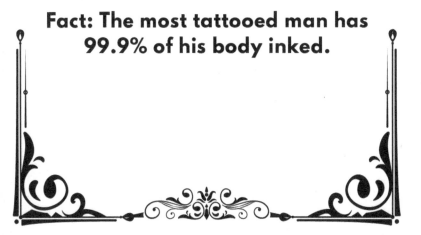

FACT 43

The world's largest yo-yo is over 11 feet in diameter.

FACT 44

The most balloons blown up in one hour is 910.

FACT 45

The record for the most eggs balanced on the back of the hand is 18.

FACT 43

The longest journey in a
pumpkin boat (yes, a real
pumpkin) covered 25.5 miles on
a river.

FACT 44

The fastest time to wrap a
person in cling film is 1 minute
and 57 seconds.

FACT 45

The most apples held in the
mouth and cut by a chainsaw in
one minute is 21.

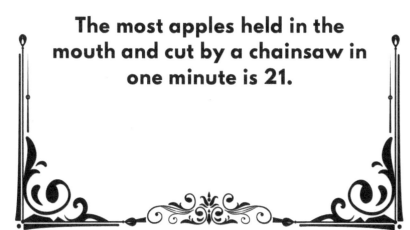

Absurd Animal Antics

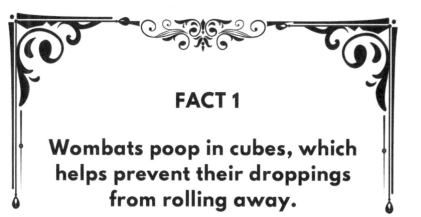

FACT 1

Wombats poop in cubes, which helps prevent their droppings from rolling away.

FACT 2

Octopuses have three hearts, and two of them stop beating when they swim

FACT 3

A group of flamingos is called a "flamboyance."

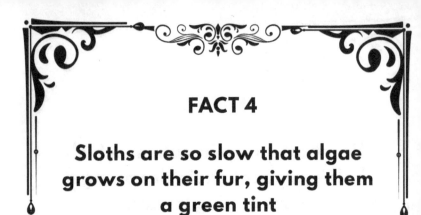

FACT 4

Sloths are so slow that algae grows on their fur, giving them a green tint

FACT 5

Sea otters hold hands while they sleep to avoid drifting apart in the water.

FACT 6

Male seahorses, not females, carry and give birth to babies.

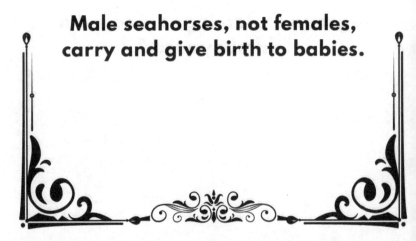

FACT 7

Cows have best friends and get stressed when they're separated.

FACT 8

Kangaroos can't walk backward.

FACT 9

Penguins propose to their mates by giving them a pebble.

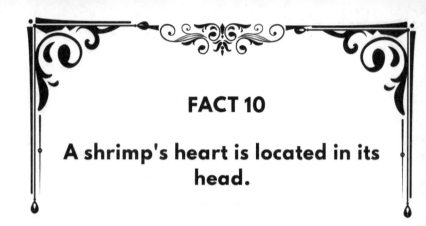

FACT 10

A shrimp's heart is located in its head.

FACT 11

Elephants are the only animals that can't jump.

FACT 12

Frogs can throw up their entire stomachs, then clean them off and swallow them again.

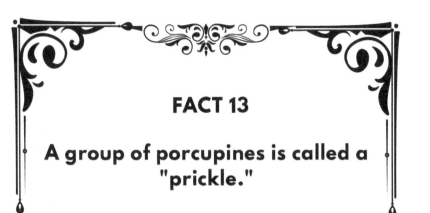

FACT 13

A group of porcupines is called a "prickle."

FACT 14

Some species of ants can create living rafts by linking their bodies together during floods.

FACT 15

Koalas sleep up to 22 hours a day and spend most of their waking hours eating.

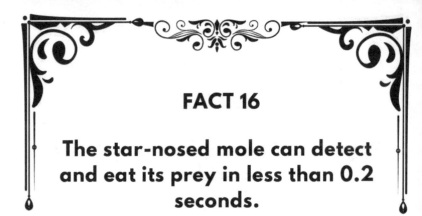

FACT 16

The star-nosed mole can detect and eat its prey in less than 0.2 seconds.

FACT 17

Giraffes have the same number of neck vertebrae as humans— just seven—but they're 10 inches long each.

FACT 18

The peacock mantis shrimp punches so fast it can break glass and boil water.

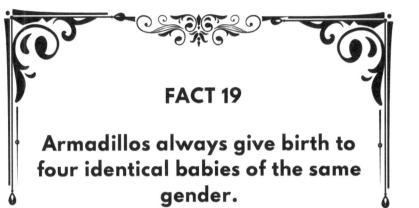

FACT 19

Armadillos always give birth to four identical babies of the same gender.

FACT 20

Owls can't move their eyeballs, which is why they have to turn their entire head to look around.

FACT 21

The immortal jellyfish can revert to its juvenile state after becoming an adult, essentially living forever—unless eaten.

FACT 22

A snail can sleep for up to three years.

FACT 23

Crocodiles can't stick out their tongues.

FACT 24

Some squirrels pretend to bury their food to trick other animals watching them.

FACT 25

The loudest animal relative to its size is the water boatman, a tiny insect that can make sounds up to 99 decibels by rubbing its penis on its abdomen.

FACT 26

Horses and cows sleep standing up but can only dream when lying down.

FACT 27

A group of crows is called a "murder."

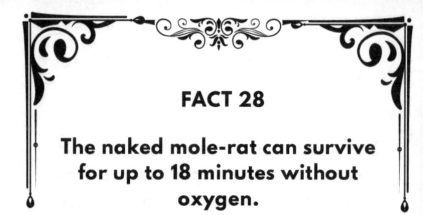

FACT 28

The naked mole-rat can survive
for up to 18 minutes without
oxygen.

FACT 29

Pigeons can do math.
Researchers found they can
learn abstract numerical rules.

FACT 30

Elephants have been known to
mourn their dead, showing signs
of grief and sometimes even
holding "funeral" gatherings.

FACT 31

The mimic octopus can impersonate 15 different marine species, including lionfish, flatfish, and sea snakes.

FACT 32

Penguins are known to "prostitute" themselves by trading pebbles for mating privileges.

FACT 33

Dragonflies are such efficient predators that they catch 95% of the prey they hunt.

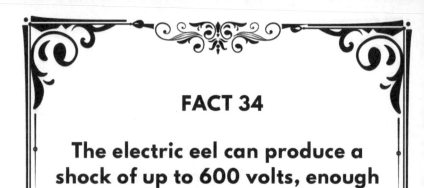

FACT 34

The electric eel can produce a shock of up to 600 volts, enough to stun a horse.

FACT 35

The slow loris is one of the few venomous mammals, delivering venom through a bite.

FACT 36

Tardigrades, also known as water bears, can survive extreme conditions, including the vacuum of space.

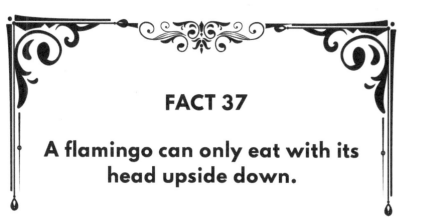

FACT 37

A flamingo can only eat with its head upside down.

FACT 38

Polar bears have black skin under their white fur to absorb heat from the sun.

FACT 39

Some fish can change gender, such as the clownfish, where the dominant male becomes female if the current female dies.

FACT 40

The aye-aye lemur uses its long middle finger to tap on trees and listen for insect larvae inside, then digs them out to eat.

FACT 41

The giant Pacific octopus has three hearts and nine brains.

FACT 42

Male giraffes determine if a female is ready to mate by tasting her urine.

FACT 43

The peregrine falcon is the fastest animal, capable of diving at speeds of over 240 miles per hour.

FACT 44

The horned lizard can squirt blood from its eyes to deter predators.

FACT 45

Some goats faint when they're startled due to a genetic condition called myotonia congenita.

FACT 46

The blobfish was voted the "world's ugliest animal," but its squishy appearance only happens out of water due to pressure changes.

FACT 47

Male emperor penguins lose up to half their body weight while incubating their eggs in freezing conditions.

FACT 48

Dolphins have names for each other and can remember these "names" for years.

Human Body Wonders

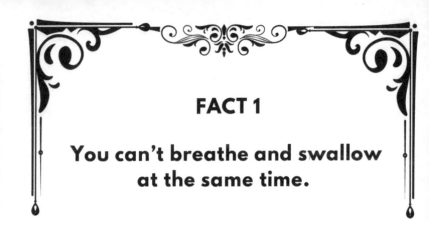

FACT 1

You can't breathe and swallow at the same time.

FACT 2

The human nose can detect over 1 trillion different scents.

FACT 3

Your body contains enough fat to make seven bars of soap.

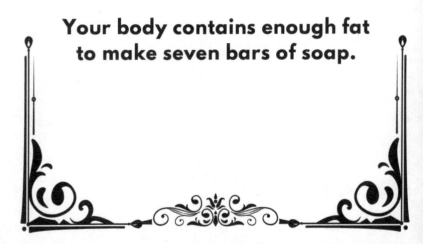

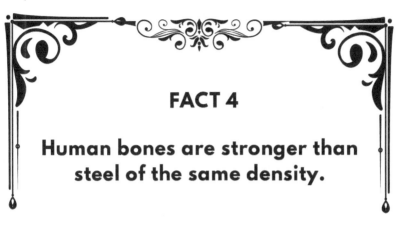

FACT 4

Human bones are stronger than
steel of the same density.

FACT 5

Your stomach gets a new lining
every three to four days to
prevent it from digesting itself.

FACT 6

The human eye can distinguish
about 10 million different colors.

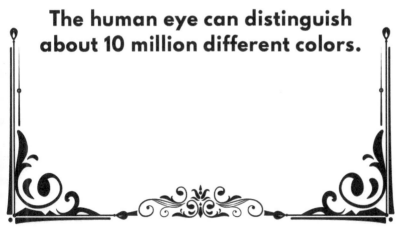

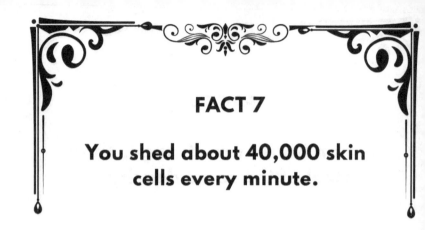

FACT 7

You shed about 40,000 skin cells every minute.

FACT 8

The human brain generates enough electricity to power a small light bulb.

FACT 9

Humans glow in the dark, but the light is too faint for our eyes to see.

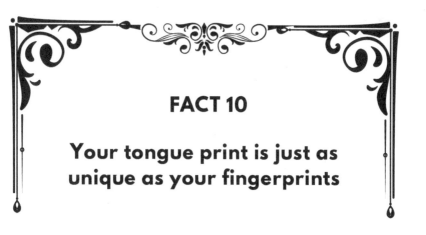

FACT 10

Your tongue print is just as unique as your fingerprints

FACT 11

Your body contains enough iron to make a small nail.

FACT 12

The human heart pumps enough blood to fill an Olympic-sized swimming pool over a lifetime.

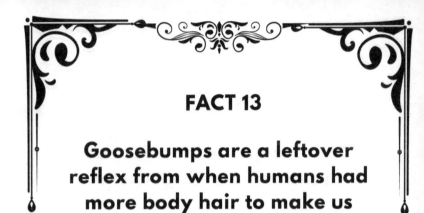

FACT 13

Goosebumps are a leftover reflex from when humans had more body hair to make us appear larger to predators.

FACT 14

You produce about a liter of mucus per day.

FACT 15

A sneeze can travel up to 100 miles per hour.

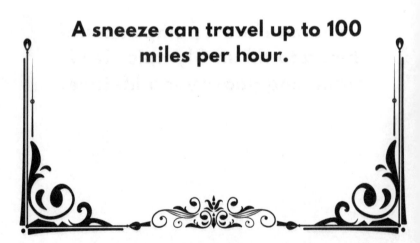

FACT 16

The fastest muscle in your body is the one that makes you blink —about 10,000 times a day.

FACT 17

The human body contains 37.2 trillion cells.

FACT 18

Your body produces enough heat in 30 minutes to boil a gallon of water.

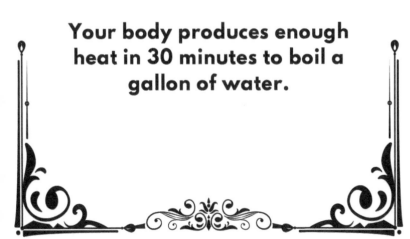

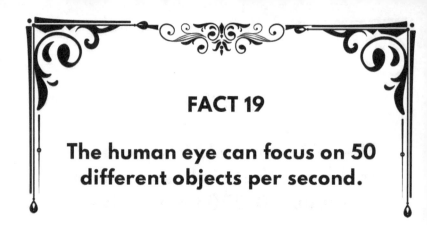

FACT 19

The human eye can focus on 50 different objects per second.

FACT 20

Your ears and nose never stop growing throughout your life.

FACT 21

The human skeleton renews itself completely every 10 years.

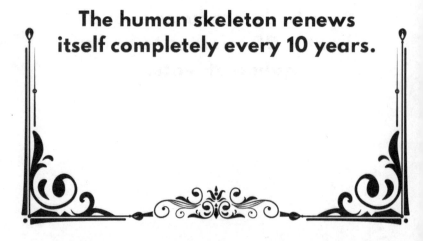

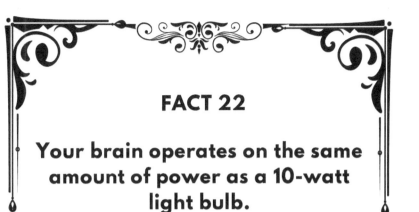

FACT 22

Your brain operates on the same amount of power as a 10-watt light bulb.

FACT 23

Your mouth is home to more bacteria than there are people on Earth.

FACT 24

The longest hiccuping spree lasted 68 years.

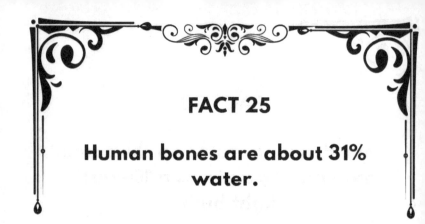

FACT 25

Human bones are about 31% water.

FACT 26

The cornea of the eye is the only part of the body without a blood supply—it gets oxygen directly from the air.

FACT 27

A human sneeze can eject particles at a speed of 100 mph.

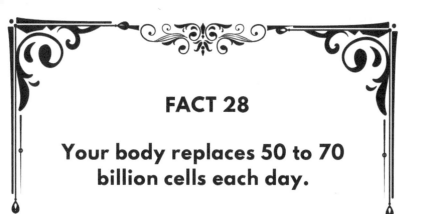

FACT 28

Your body replaces 50 to 70 billion cells each day.

FACT 29

The human brain uses about 20% of your total oxygen and energy.

FACT 30

Your body has more bacteria than human cells, with a ratio of about 10:1.

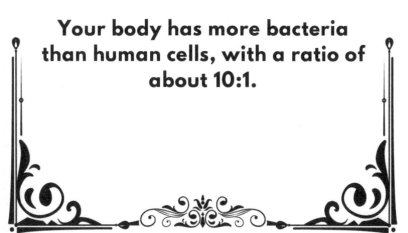

FACT 31

**A human's small intestine is
about 20 feet long.**

FACT 32

**The left lung is smaller than the
right lung to make room for
your heart.**

FACT 33

**Your pinky finger provides 50%
of your hand's strength.**

FACT 34

The human body produces about 25,000 quarts of saliva in a lifetime—enough to fill two swimming pools.

FACT 35

The human body has over 600 muscles, but the strongest muscle by size is the jaw (masseter).

FACT 36

Your taste buds are replaced every 10 to 14 days.

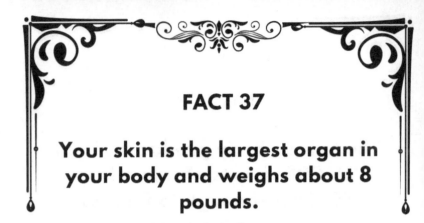

FACT 37

Your skin is the largest organ in your body and weighs about 8 pounds.

FACT 38

Your blood vessels are long enough to circle the Earth twice.

FACT 39

You produce about half a liter of sweat each day, even without exercising.

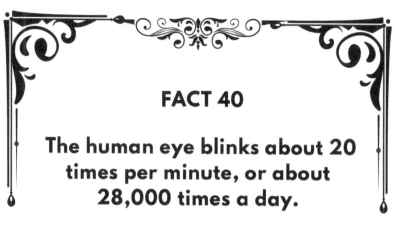

FACT 40

The human eye blinks about 20
times per minute, or about
28,000 times a day.

FACT 41

Your stomach acid is strong
enough to dissolve razor blades.

FACT 42

The human brain can store up to
2.5 petabytes of data—that's 1
million gigabytes.

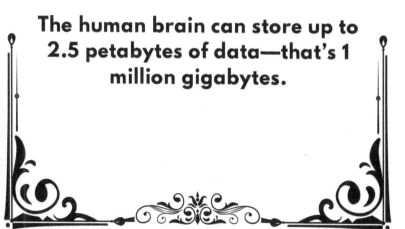

FACT 43

The longest recorded hair on a human head was over 18 feet long.

FACT 44

A single human hair can support up to 3.5 ounces of weight.

FACT 45

The human heart beats about 100,000 times a day.

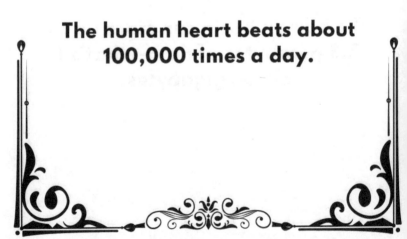

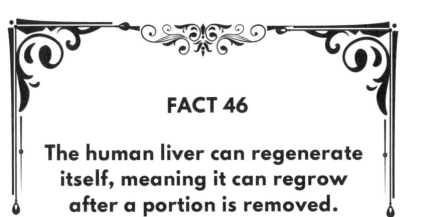

FACT 46

The human liver can regenerate itself, meaning it can regrow after a portion is removed.

FACT 47

It takes about 17 muscles to smile and 43 to frown.

FACT 48

Your body contains enough carbon to make about 9,000 pencils.

Crazy Sports
You Won't Believe Exist

FACT 1

In Finland, there's a Wife Carrying Championship where the winner earns their wife's weight in beer.

FACT 2

Chess Boxing is a real sport where participants alternate between boxing rounds and chess matches.

FACT 3

In England, there's a Cheese Rolling competition where participants chase a wheel of cheese down a steep hill.

FACT 4

Toe Wrestling is a competitive sport in the UK, where opponents lock toes and try to pin each other's foot down.

FACT 5

In Japan, there's a sport called Bo-Taoshi, where teams of 75 compete to knock down a pole defended by the other team.

FACT 6

Underwater Hockey, also known as Octopush, is played at the bottom of a swimming pool with players holding their breath.

FACT 7

Ferret Legging involves competitors stuffing live ferrets down their trousers and enduring the discomfort for as long as possible.

FACT 8

Extreme Ironing is an actual sport where participants iron clothes in extreme environments like cliffs or underwater.

FACT 9

In Australia, there's a Camel Racing Championship where camels, not horses, are the stars of the race.

FACT 10

Bog Snorkeling is a sport where competitors race through water-filled ditches while wearing snorkels and flippers.

FACT 11

Unicycle Hockey is exactly what it sounds like—playing hockey on unicycles.

FACT 12

The USA holds an annual event called the Air Guitar World Championships, where participants "play" guitar with no instruments.

FACT 13

In Switzerland, Hornussen is a traditional sport where players hit a puck, called a "Nouss," and others try to knock it down with long sticks.

FACT 14

The Redneck Games in Georgia include events like mud pit belly flops, bobbing for pigs' feet, and toilet seat throwing.

FACT 15

In Ireland, there's a sport called Hurling, one of the oldest field games, where players use sticks to hit a ball into a goal.

FACT 16

Car Curling is a sport in Russia where teams push small cars on ice to a target, just like curling with stones.

FACT 17

Turkey Bowling is a sport in which frozen turkeys are used to knock down bowling pins.

FACT 18

In Spain, participants engage in Baby Jumping, where men dressed as devils leap over babies lying on mattresses.

FACT 19

In America, there's an annual Frog Jumping Contest where the frog that jumps the furthest wins.

FACT 20

Zorbing is a sport where participants roll downhill inside a giant inflatable ball.

FACT 21

In the UK, there's a sport called Conkers, where contestants try to break their opponent's horse chestnut on a string.

FACT 22

In Venezuela, competitive hair growing is a sport, and participants take pride in having the longest hair possible.

FACT 23

The Rock Paper Scissors World Championship is a real event where participants face off in a battle of hands.

FACT 24

Shin Kicking, where opponents kick each other's shins to force a fall, is a competitive sport in England.

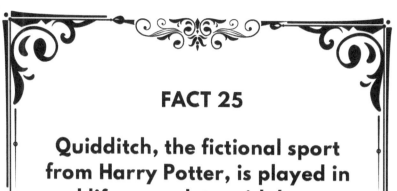

FACT 25

Quidditch, the fictional sport from Harry Potter, is played in real life, complete with brooms between the players' legs.

FACT 26

In Thailand, Kite Fighting is a sport where competitors try to cut their opponents' kite strings.

FACT 27

In Italy, there's a sport called Calcio Storico, a mix of soccer, rugby, and wrestling, often resulting in violent matches.

FACT 28

Giant Pumpkin Kayaking is a sport in Canada where participants carve out pumpkins and use them as kayaks to race across water.

FACT 29

The World Sauna Championships in Finland involve sitting in a sauna until the last person passes out or leaves.

FACT 30

Chess Boxing, a combination of chess and boxing, tests both mental and physical strength in a unique way.

FACT 31

In the Philippines, there's a sport called Sepak Takraw, where players kick a rattan ball over a net using only their feet, knees, and head.

FACT 32

In New Zealand, competitors race down steep hills in Bathtub Racing, where bathtubs are fitted with engines and used as boats.

FACT 33

Buzkashi is the national sport of Afghanistan, where players on horseback drag a goat carcass toward a goal.

FACT 34

In the Netherlands, Fierljeppen is a sport where participants pole vault over canals.

FACT 35

Competitive Dog Surfing involves dogs riding surfboards on waves, with the best rider being crowned the winner.

FACT 36

In Scotland, the Caber Toss is a traditional event where participants toss a large log end-over-end.

FACT 37

The Marathon des Sables is an ultramarathon in the Sahara Desert, covering over 150 miles in extreme heat.

FACT 38

In Alaska, the World Eskimo-Indian Olympics feature events like ear pulling, where participants pull on each other's ears until one gives up.

FACT 39

In Thailand, Elephant Polo is a sport where players ride elephants and use long mallets to hit the ball.

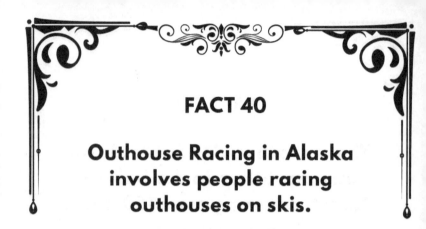

FACT 40

Outhouse Racing in Alaska involves people racing outhouses on skis.

FACT 41

In the UK, there's a sport called Mud Racing, where participants race vehicles through thick mud.

FACT 42

The Ig Nobel Prizes include awards for quirky achievements, and there's even a sport for finding the silliest "scientific" studies.

FACT 43

In Canada, snowball fighting is
an organized sport called
Yukigassen, with specific rules
and tournaments.

FACT 44

In India, Mallakhamb is a
traditional sport where
gymnasts perform yoga-like
poses on a pole.

FACT 45

Bus Pulling is a sport where
competitors pull buses with their
bare hands in the fastest time.

FACT 46

In the UK, Extreme Croquet is played with obstacles like hills, mud, and streams.

FACT 47

Worm Charming is a sport in which participants tap the ground to "charm" worms out of the soil.

FACT 48

In Germany, Finger Wrestling is a competitive sport where two participants try to pull each other across a table using only their fingers.

Unbeliavable Inventions

FACT 1

The Hula Chair is a chair that wiggles your hips for you, designed as a fitness tool to simulate hula hooping while sitting.

FACT 2

The baby cage was invented in 1922 to hang babies out of apartment windows for fresh air.

FACT 3

In the 1980s, Clippy, Microsoft's paperclip assistant, was introduced as a digital helper, but it annoyed users so much it was discontinued.

FACT 4

The pet rock was one of the most successful novelty toys of the 1970s, consisting of literally a rock in a box.

FACT 5

The Segway was hyped as a revolutionary mode of transportation but failed to catch on, mostly due to its awkwardness.

FACT 6

The Snuggie, a blanket with sleeves, was a huge success despite looking ridiculous, with millions sold worldwide.

FACT 7

Doggles are goggles made specifically for dogs to protect their eyes from sunlight and debris.

FACT 8

The Shower Mic is a waterproof microphone for people who love singing in the shower.

FACT 9

Anti-pervert hairy stockings were invented in China to deter unwanted attention by making legs appear hairy.

FACT 10

The Butter Stick is butter packaged like a glue stick so you can spread it more easily.

FACT 11

In 2009, Bic launched a pen designed specifically for women, sparking outrage because it seemed unnecessary and sexist.

FACT 12

The Flying Car has been in development since the 1940s, but none have been mass-produced or truly successful.

FACT 13

The banana slicer is a plastic tool created to cut bananas into perfect slices—although a knife works just fine

FACT 14

The pizza scissors are a combination of scissors and a spatula to cut and serve pizza slices more easily.

FACT 15

The USB Pet Rock was an updated version of the pet rock that did nothing but sit on your desk, without even needing a USB connection.

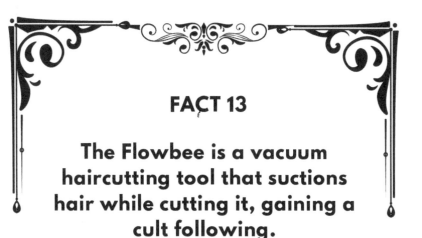

FACT 13

The Flowbee is a vacuum haircutting tool that suctions hair while cutting it, gaining a cult following.

FACT 14

Invisible Ink Pens were invented for writing secret messages that only become visible under UV light.

FACT 15

The Nose Stylus is a tool designed for people who want to use their smartphone while their hands are occupied.

FACT 16

The Toaster Printer prints designs on toast, allowing you to have patterns or images on your breakfast.

FACT 17

The Fliz bike is a bicycle without pedals or a seat; riders hang from a harness and run to propel themselves.

FACT 18

The Baby Mop is a onesie with mop-like fibers on the stomach and arms, so babies can clean the floor as they crawl.

FACT 19

The Toaster Printer prints
designs on toast, allowing you
to have patterns or images on
your breakfast.

FACT 20

The Fliz bike is a bicycle without
pedals or a seat; riders hang
from a harness and run to
propel themselves.

FACT 21

The Baby Mop is a onesie with
mop-like fibers on the stomach
and arms, so babies can clean
the floor as they crawl.

FACT 22

TwitterPeek was a device invented solely to tweet, but it failed when smartphones became popular.

FACT 23

The Selfie Toaster allows users to toast their own face onto a slice of bread.

FACT 24

The Finger Fork is a mini fork that slips onto your finger, so you can stab and eat food without utensils.

FACT 25

The Bacon Alarm Clock wakes you up by cooking bacon, so you smell breakfast the moment you open your eyes.

FACT 26

Canned Air is literally air in a can, marketed as a luxury item in some polluted cities.

FACT 27

The Umbrella Drone follows you around to keep you dry without you having to hold it.

FACT 28

The Tamagotchi was a digital pet that became a massive fad in the 1990s, requiring users to "feed" and "care" for it virtually.

FACT 29

The Wake n' Bacon alarm clock automatically cooks bacon for you to wake up to the smell of sizzling breakfast.

FACT 30

Cuddle Pillows shaped like arms or body parts were invented for people who want to simulate hugging someone while they sleep.

FACT 31

Heated Butter Knife warms up to help you spread butter more easily.

FACT 32

The Necomimi Cat Ears are brainwave-controlled cat ears that move according to your emotions, designed for cosplay and fun.

FACT 33

Nap Desks allow you to lie down for a nap at work without leaving your desk.

FACT 34

Licki Brush is a giant, tongue-shaped brush you hold in your mouth to groom your cat like a mother cat would.

FACT 35

The Motorized Ice Cream Cone rotates the ice cream for you so you can lick it without turning the cone.

FACT 36

The Pocket Fish Pen is a tiny fishing rod that collapses down into the size of a pen, but works as a fully functional fishing pole.

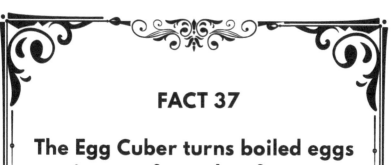

FACT 37

The Egg Cuber turns boiled eggs into perfect cubes for no apparent reason other than visual appeal.

FACT 38

The iPotty is a potty training toilet with a built-in iPad stand to keep kids entertained while they learn.

FACT 39

Sleeping Bag Suits are wearable sleeping bags designed for people who want to stay warm while walking or lounging outdoors.

FACT 40

Potato Flavored Soda was created in Japan and actually tasted like real potatoes— unsurprisingly, it didn't take off.

FACT 41

Dog Translator Collars claim to translate your dog's barks into human language, though most results are questionable at best.

FACT 42

Goggle Umbrellas have transparent hoods that completely cover your head so you can see where you're going without getting wet.

FACT 43

The NoPhone is a plastic rectangle designed to feel like a phone in your hand, made for people addicted to their phones but wanting to quit.

FACT 44

The Hamster Shredder combines a hamster wheel and paper shredder, so your hamster powers the shredder by running.

FACT 45

The Wrist-Mounted Toilet Paper Holder lets you wear a roll of toilet paper on your wrist, for people constantly in need of a tissue.

FACT 46

The Sound Asleep Pillow has built-in speakers, allowing you to listen to music or white noise while lying on it.

FACT 47

Fart Filtering Underwear was invented to help people avoid embarrassing moments by neutralizing unpleasant odors.

FACT 48

The Car Exhaust Grill is a cooking device that attaches to your car's exhaust pipe and grills food while you drive.

History Weirdest Moments

FACT 1

In 1838, Edgar Allan Poe wrote a story about four shipwreck survivors who ate a cabin boy. Years later, a real shipwreck occurred, and the survivors did the same, naming the boy Richard Parker—just like in Poe's story.

FACT 2

Napoleon Bonaparte was once attacked by a horde of bunnies during a rabbit hunt when hundreds of rabbits charged at him.

FACT 3

In 1923, jockey Frank Hayes won a horse race despite having died mid-race from a heart attack. His body remained in the saddle until the horse crossed the finish line.

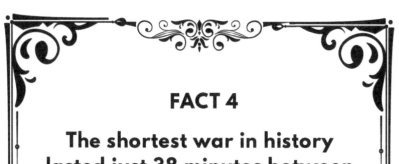

FACT 4

The shortest war in history lasted just 38 minutes between Britain and Zanzibar in 1896.

FACT 5

During World War II, a "Great Emu War" was fought in Australia—between soldiers and emus. The emus won.

FACT 6

Roman Emperor Caligula once declared war on the sea. He ordered his soldiers to collect seashells as "spoils of war."

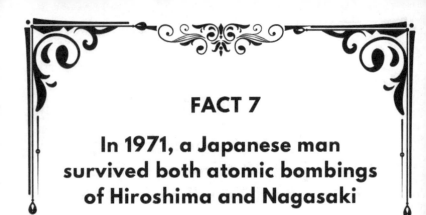

FACT 7

In 1971, a Japanese man survived both atomic bombings of Hiroshima and Nagasaki

FACT 8

Cleopatra lived closer in time to the Moon landing than to the construction of the Great Pyramid of Giza.

FACT 9

In the 1800s, dentures were often made from the teeth of dead soldiers.

FACT 10

In 1849, an Austrian tailor named Franz Reichelt jumped off the Eiffel Tower wearing a parachute suit he invented. It didn't work.

FACT 11

In 1920, Babe Ruth once hit a 587-foot home run, one of the longest ever recorded.

FACT 12

During the American Civil War, soldiers would exchange coffee and tobacco across battle lines during ceasefires.

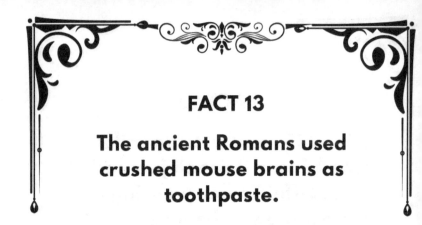

FACT 13

The ancient Romans used crushed mouse brains as toothpaste.

FACT 14

In 1859, the U.S. and the UK almost went to war over a pig that was shot in the Pacific Northwest, known as the Pig War.

FACT 15

The shortest-reigning pope in history was Pope Urban VII, who reigned for just 13 days in 1590.

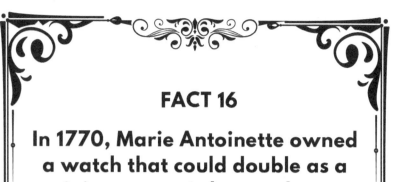

FACT 16

In 1770, Marie Antoinette owned a watch that could double as a miniature music box and even play small symphonies.

FACT 17

The Leaning Tower of Pisa has been leaning since its construction began in the 12th century due to soft ground.

FACT 18

The Guinness World Record for the longest reigning monarch is held by King Louis XIV of France, who ruled for 72 years.

FACT 19

In the 16th century, people believed that the powder from ground-up mummies had healing powers, and it was sold as medicine.

FACT 20

In 1938, British Prime Minister Neville Chamberlain gave Hitler a toy bulldog as a peace offering.

FACT 21

In ancient China, people used to eat tea leaves compressed into bricks, which also served as currency.

FACT 22

During the Victorian era, some women wore dresses so wide they couldn't fit through doorways.

FACT 23

Genghis Khan's empire was so vast that 1 in 200 men today are believed to be his descendants.

FACT 24

President Andrew Jackson once had a 1,400-pound block of cheese delivered to the White House and invited the public to eat it.

FACT 25

During World War II, the British government considered releasing glue-covered balloons over Germany to cause chaos.

FACT 26

When President Abraham Lincoln was assassinated, his bodyguard was at a nearby saloon instead of guarding him.

FACT 27

During Prohibition in the U.S., some moonshiners wore cow shoes to disguise their footprints and avoid detection.

FACT 28

King Henry VIII once spent what would now be $18 million on a single New Year's party in 1541.

FACT 29

In 1922, the world's longest hiccuping spree began. Charles Osborne hiccupped for 68 years straight.

FACT 30

Thomas Jefferson invented the swivel chair, a revolutionary innovation for the time.

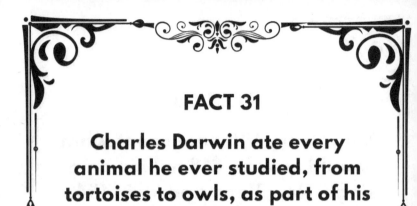

FACT 31

Charles Darwin ate every animal he ever studied, from tortoises to owls, as part of his research.

FACT 32

In ancient Greece, wearing a fake beard was a serious crime.

FACT 33

The Aztecs used cacao beans as currency, and sometimes people were paid in chocolate.

FACT 34

In the 18th century, French women wore enormous wigs that were sometimes more than two feet tall, with live birds perched in them.

FACT 35

During World War I, British soldiers were given "trench coats" to wear, which became fashionable after the war.

FACT 36

The Aztecs used cacao beans as currency, and In 1839, British aristocrats threw parties where they inhaled laughing gas for fun. sometimes people were paid in chocolate.

FACT 37

The world's first selfie was taken in 1839 by Robert Cornelius, who set up his camera and sat for over a minute to capture the image.

FACT 38

In the 1700s, Russian Empress Catherine the Great ordered her servants to tickle her feet while she ate dinner to improve her digestion.

FACT 39

The famous Egyptian pharaoh Ramses II fathered over 100 children.

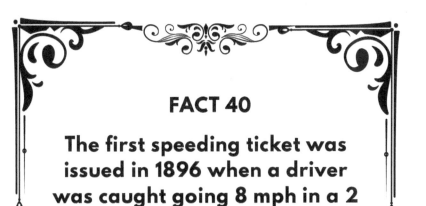

FACT 40

The first speeding ticket was issued in 1896 when a driver was caught going 8 mph in a 2 mph zone.

FACT 41

The first recorded instance of a human streaker was in 1799, when a man ran naked through London's streets as a bet.

FACT 42

In 16th-century France, some men wore codpieces stuffed with padding to exaggerate their "manhood" for fashion.

FACT 43

Alexander the Great was once offered an island as a gift but refused it because it "wasn't big enough."

FACT 44

In 1911, a man stole the Mona Lisa from the Louvre by hiding in a broom closet overnight.

FACT 45

Winston Churchill was once hit by a car in New York City because he looked the wrong way when crossing the street.

FACT 46

During the Middle Ages, people thought that donkeys could cure toothaches by eating the leaves from a donkey's favorite plant.

FACT 47

The first electric traffic light was installed in 1914 in Cleveland, Ohio.

FACT 48

In ancient Rome, salt was so valuable that soldiers were sometimes paid in salt instead of money, leading to the word "salary."

FACT 1

Honey is the only food that never spoils. Archaeologists have found pots of honey in ancient Egyptian tombs that are over 3,000 years old and still edible.

FACT 2

Ketchup was originally sold as medicine in the 1830s.

FACT 3

The most stolen food in the world is cheese, with about 4% of all cheese being stolen globally.

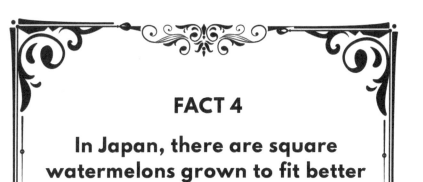

FACT 4

In Japan, there are square watermelons grown to fit better in refrigerators.

FACT 5

Cashews grow on the bottom of a fruit, and the nuts are actually seeds.

FACT 6

The world's most expensive pizza costs over $12,000 and is topped with three types of caviar and edible gold.

FACT 7

Bananas are berries, but strawberries aren't.

FACT 8

There is a fruit called the "Miracle Berry" that makes sour foods taste sweet after you eat it.

FACT 9

Apples float in water because 25% of their volume is air.

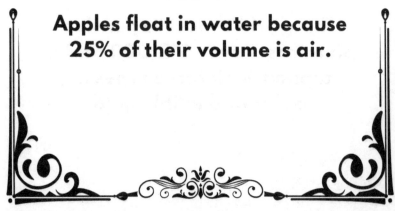

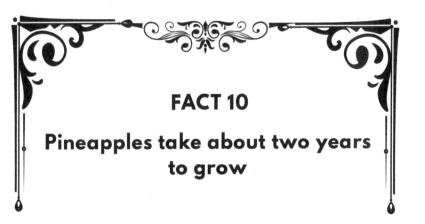

FACT 10

Pineapples take about two years to grow

FACT 11

Lobsters used to be considered "poor man's food" and were fed to prisoners in colonial America.

FACT 12

You can make diamonds from peanut butter—scientists have used high-pressure techniques to turn peanut butter into a diamond.

FACT 13

The popsicle was invented by an 11-year-old who left soda outside overnight with a stick in it.

FACT 14

Carrots were originally purple, not orange.

FACT 15

In 2013, Nutella caused a massive traffic jam in Germany when 5,000 jars spilled across a highway.

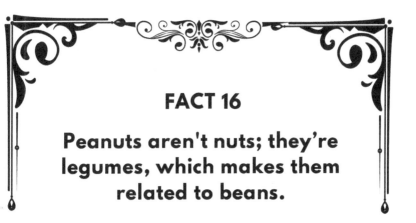

FACT 16

Peanuts aren't nuts; they're legumes, which makes them related to beans.

FACT 17

In South Korea, there's a popular drink called "Sikhye" made from fermented rice.

FACT 18

In Iceland, they eat a dish called hákarl, which is fermented shark that has been buried for months.

FACT 19

Tomatoes were once considered poisonous because they are part of the nightshade family.

FACT 20

A single portobello mushroom can contain more potassium than a banana.

FACT 21

The largest chocolate bar ever made weighed over 12,000 pounds.

FACT 22

Butterflies actually "taste" with their feet.

FACT 23

Some people in Italy enjoy a special kind of cheese, called "Casu Marzu," which contains live maggots.

FACT 24

The Hawaiian pizza was invented in Canada, not Hawaii.

FACT 25

There's a type of coffee made from beans that have been eaten and excreted by civet cats, known as "kopi luwak."

FACT 26

The Guinness World Record for the largest sushi roll weighed over 6,000 pounds.

FACT 27

The world's hottest chili pepper is so spicy that it can cause your skin to blister upon contact.

FACT 28

The Kit Kat in Japan comes in over 300 flavors, including wasabi, green tea, and baked potato.

FACT 29

Worcestershire sauce is made from dissolved anchovies.

FACT 30

In 2001, a woman tried to sue McDonald's after burning herself on a pickle from a hot hamburger.

FACT 31

Cows produce more milk when they listen to slow music.

FACT 32

During World War II, ketchup was sold as a substitute for tomatoes, which were rationed.

FACT 33

A Swedish fish farm accidentally bred fish that taste like bacon.

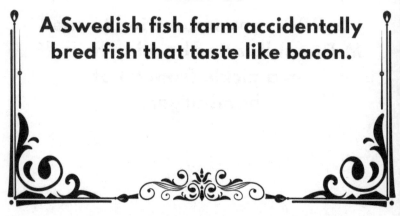

FACT 34

The tradition of birthday cakes with candles originated from the Greeks, who would place candles on moon-shaped cakes for the goddess Artemis.

FACT 35

McDonald's once made bubblegum-flavored broccoli to encourage kids to eat healthier. It didn't work.

FACT 36

The color orange was named after the fruit, not the other way around.

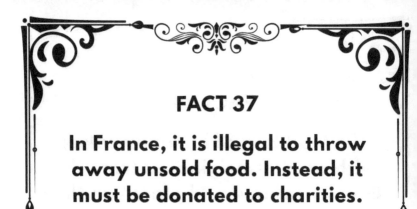

FACT 37

In France, it is illegal to throw away unsold food. Instead, it must be donated to charities.

FACT 38

Coconut water can be used as a substitute for blood plasma in emergencies because it has a similar composition.

FACT 39

The world's largest pizza was made in Rome and covered 13,580 square feet.

FACT 40

In Japan, people eat fried maple leaves as a snack.

FACT 41

Peaches and nectarines are essentially the same fruit—the only difference is the fuzz on the peach.

FACT 42

Coconuts kill more people each year than sharks do.

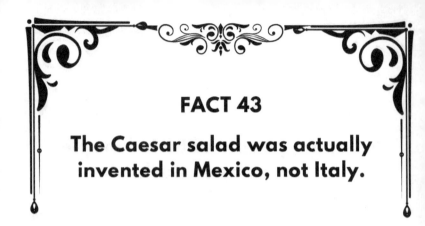

FACT 43

The Caesar salad was actually invented in Mexico, not Italy.

FACT 44

Watermelons are 92% water, which is why they are so hydrating.

FACT 45

In the 1800s, ketchup was sold as a cure for indigestion.

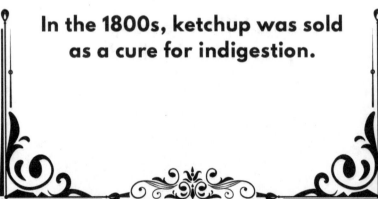

FACT 46

One of the world's most expensive desserts is a $25,000 ice cream sundae covered in edible 23-karat gold.

FACT 47

Cranberries can bounce when they are ripe

FACT 48

Eating too many carrots can turn your skin orange due to the high amount of beta-carotene.

FACT 1

In 1815, the eruption of Mount Tambora in Indonesia caused "The Year Without a Summer," leading to global crop failures and food shortages.

FACT 2

There is a desert in Antarctica—the driest place on Earth, with no rain for nearly 2 million years.

FACT 3

Fire whirls, or "fire tornadoes," can occur when intense heat and wind combine during a wildfire, creating a swirling vortex of flame.

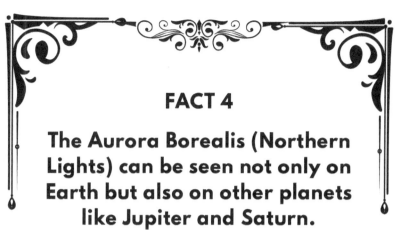

FACT 4

The Aurora Borealis (Northern Lights) can be seen not only on Earth but also on other planets like Jupiter and Saturn.

FACT 5

The Aurora Borealis (Northern Lights) can be seen not only on Earth but also on other planets like Jupiter and Saturn.

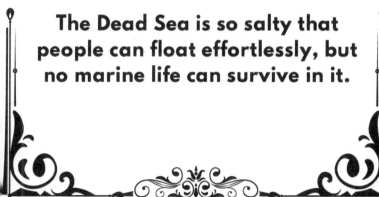

FACT 6

The Dead Sea is so salty that people can float effortlessly, but no marine life can survive in it.

FACT 7

"Blood Falls" in Antarctica is a red-colored waterfall caused by iron-rich water oxidizing as it flows out of a glacier.

FACT 8

Lightning strikes the Earth about 100 times per second on average, adding up to over 8 million strikes per day.

FACT 9

There is a continuous lightning storm in Venezuela called "Catatumbo Lightning," occurring up to 260 nights a year.

FACT 10

The longest recorded rainbow lasted nearly 9 hours in Taiwan.

FACT 11

Volcanic lightning occurs when ash particles from a volcanic eruption collide, creating electrical charges.

FACT 12

Bioluminescent waves, where the sea glows at night, are caused by microorganisms like plankton lighting up when disturbed.

FACT 13

There is a "Door to Hell" in Turkmenistan, a natural gas field that has been burning since 1971.

FACT 14

A megaflash of lightning once stretched over 477 miles, the longest single lightning bolt ever recorded.

FACT 15

The Atacama Desert in Chile is so dry that some areas have never recorded any rainfall.

FACT 16

Venus flytraps, native to North Carolina, can snap shut on prey in less than a second.

FACT 17

The blue whale is the largest animal ever known, growing up to 100 feet long and weighing as much as 200 tons.

FACT 18

The Great Barrier Reef, the largest living structure on Earth, can be seen from space.

FACT 19

There are "rivers in the sky"—atmospheric rivers carrying huge amounts of water vapor, often causing massive flooding when they hit land.

FACT 20

The Grand Canyon was formed over millions of years by the Colorado River carving through rock layers.

FACT 21

There are places on Earth where it rains fish, such as in Honduras, where fish mysteriously fall from the sky during heavy storms.

FACT 22

The world's oldest tree, a bristlecone pine in California, is over 4,800 years old

FACT 23

The coldest temperature ever recorded on Earth was -128.6°F (-89.2°C) in Antarctica.

FACT 24

There are more trees on Earth than stars in the Milky Way galaxy—about 3 trillion trees versus 100-400 billion stars.

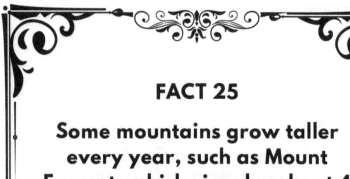

FACT 25

Some mountains grow taller every year, such as Mount Everest, which rises by about 4 millimeters annually.

FACT 26

The Earth's rotation is gradually slowing down, meaning that days are getting longer—about 1.7 milliseconds per century.

FACT 27

The deepest point on Earth is the Mariana Trench, which is over 36,000 feet deep—deeper than Mount Everest is tall.

FACT 28

Some mushrooms glow in the dark, using bioluminescence to attract insects that spread their spores.

FACT 29

A lake in Tanzania called Lake Natron turns animals into "stone" by preserving their bodies in hardened salt.

FACT 30

The Sahara Desert expands by about 30 miles each year due to desertification.

FACT 31

There's a waterfall in Hawaii called "Rainbow Falls" that produces a rainbow every morning if the sun hits it just right.

FACT 32

In the Amazon rainforest, it rains over 200 days a year, making it one of the wettest places on Earth.

FACT 33

There is a beach in the Maldives that glows at night due to bioluminescent plankton in the water.

FACT 34

Some animals, like the Arctic fox, can change the color of their fur depending on the season for better camouflage.

FACT 35

"Moonbows," or lunar rainbows, can occur when moonlight is reflected and refracted through raindrops.

FACT 36

Jellyfish are among the oldest living creatures, existing for more than 500 million years.

FACT 37

Salt flats in Bolivia, called Salar de Uyuni, become a giant mirror when covered in a thin layer of water.

FACT 38

In Norway, there is a natural phenomenon called the "Midnight Sun," where the sun doesn't set for several weeks in the summer.

FACT 39

The planet Venus spins backward compared to most other planets, meaning the sun rises in the west and sets in the east.

FACT 40

Earth's magnetic field is slowly shifting, and scientists predict the magnetic poles may one day flip.

FACT 41

Geysers, like Old Faithful in Yellowstone, shoot boiling water and steam into the air due to pressure from underground heat.

FACT 42

The "Sailing Stones" of Death Valley are rocks that mysteriously move across the desert floor, leaving trails behind them.

FACT 43

In Siberia, sinkholes known as "mega slumps" are rapidly expanding due to thawing permafrost, creating craters in the landscape.

FACT 44

The "Northern Lights" can sometimes be seen as far south as Scotland during particularly strong solar storms.

FACT 45

There are more volcanoes on Venus than any other planet in the solar system—over 1,600

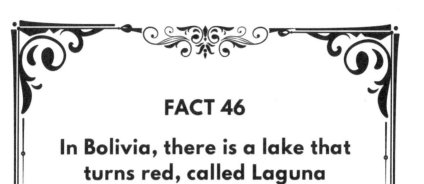

FACT 46

In Bolivia, there is a lake that turns red, called Laguna Colorada, due to red algae and sediments in the water

FACT 47

Hailstones can grow to the size of softballs during severe storms, falling at speeds of up to 100 mph.

FACT 48

Earth is the only known planet with liquid water on its surface, making it unique in the solar system.

Nature's Wildest Phenomena

Food Facts to Digest